This book is dedicated to Ellie, Greg, Mal, Will and Ali, my wonderful grandchildren.

The Story of the book

Once again I am launching a book with a close association to the bees. 'Beelicious Recipes with Honey' grew from an idea from my very good friend Maria. She said "you should compile a cookery book for kids using honey in your recipes", and here it is. In these recipes I have mentioned using local honey.

I use Belvedere Honey produced by Jim Donohue, and Paul Lynch's honey. I would recommend you use honey from your locality if possible, it is always the best.

Most of the recipes in this book are ones which my daughter-in-law Hilary and my grandchildren Ellie, Greg, Mal and Will have tried and tested many times. Ellie and her Mum along with Greg and Mal bake daily in their beautiful kitchen which Ellie calls 'Buttercup Bakery'. Will and Ali bake scones and buns regularly.

Ellie has hand written some of the recipes and I think this adds great charm to the book.

Nana D (myself) takes the credit for the smoothies.

Mary Kelly who wishes to be a pastry chef when she finishes school is the creator of the wonderful 'Gingerbread Boys & Girls'. I hope that all your cooking will be BEELICIOUS.

Published by Dbee Press,
8 New Row, Belvedere, Mullingar, Co. Westmeath, Ireland
Text copyright Dolores Keaveney 2012
Illustration copyright Dolores Keaveney 2012
Artwork copyright Dolores Keaveney 2012
All rights reserved

Design by Lucy Tormey, www.lucytormey.net
Layout & Print by Mind's i Graphic Design Ltd.
www.mindsi.ie

ISBN: 978-0-9571917-0-9

Beelicious

Recipes with Honey

Illustrated & compiled by Dolores Keaveney
www.doloreskeaveney.com
d_keaveney@yahoo.co.uk

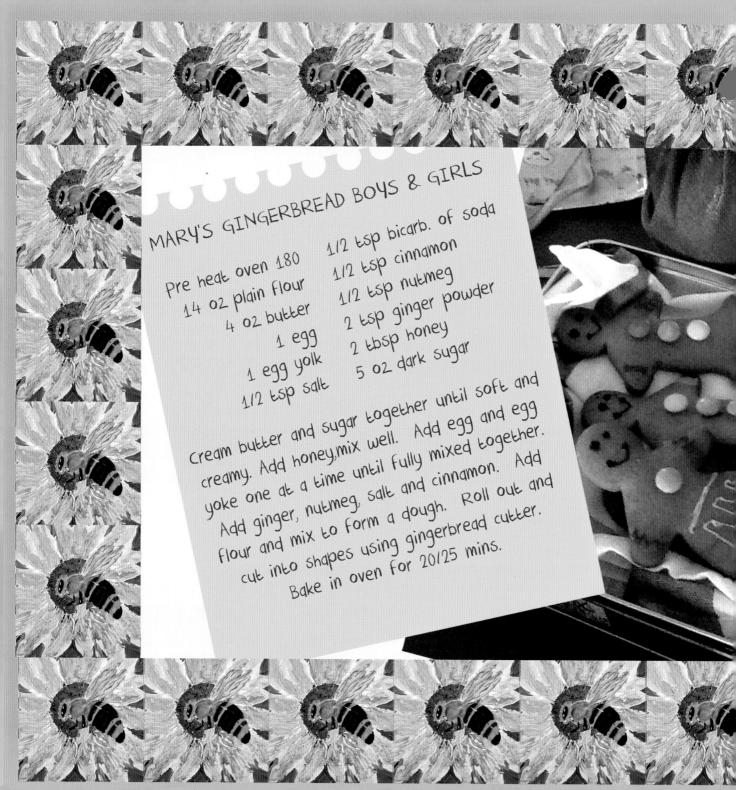

MARY'S GINGERBREAD BOYS & GIRLS

Pre heat oven 180
14 oz plain flour
4 oz butter
1 egg
1 egg yolk
1/2 tsp salt

1/2 tsp bicarb. of soda
1/2 tsp cinnamon
1/2 tsp nutmeg
2 tsp ginger powder
2 tbsp honey
5 oz dark sugar

Cream butter and sugar together until soft and creamy. Add honey, mix well. Add egg and egg yoke one at a time until fully mixed together. Add ginger, nutmeg, salt and cinnamon. Add flour and mix to form a dough. Roll out and cut into shapes using gingerbread cutter. Bake in oven for 20/25 mins.

Honeybees make beeswax

A worker honey bee visits and collects nectar from two million flowers to make one pound of honey

Will's Beelicious Blueberry Pancakes

One cup of flour
One cup of milk
One egg
Pinch of salt
Whisk together with hand whisk,
important job for little person!
Heat a little veg oil and knob of butter
in pan and drop in mixture using a ladle,
important job for big person!
Drizzle with honey and some of your
favourite berries.

HILARY'S HONEY SCONES

Preheat oven 210 degrees c

Dry Ingredients
Sieve together:
1lb of plain flour
2tsp Bextartar
1tsp bread soda
1tsp Salt &
Rub in 4 ounces
of margarine

Wet Ingredients
Mix 9fl ounces of buttermilk/milk
A beaten egg
(save a little to brush on scones
before baking)
1 tbsp of honey together in a jug

Make a well in dry ingredients and mix in
wet to make a dough using a fork
Gather into a ball
Place on floured surface and flatten with hands
(2cm thick)
Cut out and place on floured tray
Bake for 15 minutes
Dust with icing sugar

A honey bee visits 50 – 100 flowers during a collection trip

Ellie's Flapjacks

10 oz   butter

4 oz   soft brown sugar

2 tsp   honey

1½ tbsp   golden syrup

14 oz   porridge oats

Place all ingredients except oats in a saucepan and melt — don't boil!

Stir in oats

press into well greased baking tray and bake 25 minutes 180°c

Bees have long tongues that enable them to obtain nectar from the flowers

HONEY BEES have 6 legs, 2 eyes, 2 wings, a nectar pouch, and a stomach.

Boys Banana Bread

Smells great!

3 ripe bananas (mash)

4oz Sugar

2 tbsp honey

2 ½ fl.oz Veg.oil

2 tsp vanilla extract

2 eggs

Stir all wet ingredients together in a large bowl with wooden spoon

8oz Self raising flour

½ tsp Salt

¼ tsp bread soda

Add in dry ingredients and mix into batter. Pour into well greased 2lb. loaf tin and bake.

45 minutes
180°C

180°C

Ellie's Tartlets

20 minutes

180°c

Ready to Roll Puff Pastry

Cut out Shapes with cookie cutters

Place on floured baking tray
brush Pastry with egg wash
Place apple slices on Pastry

Drizzle with honey and bake

French
toast   ooh lala!   by
                    Ellie
4 eggs
3 fl.oz. Milk
Whisk together
cut bread into triangles, they fit
into pan easier

Dip bread into egg Mixture
put a little veg oil and Knob
of butter into the pan

Fry eggy bread till golden brown
on each side

Adult help needed

A colony of bees
consists of
20,000 – 60,000
honeybees and
one queen.

Ellie's beelicious buns

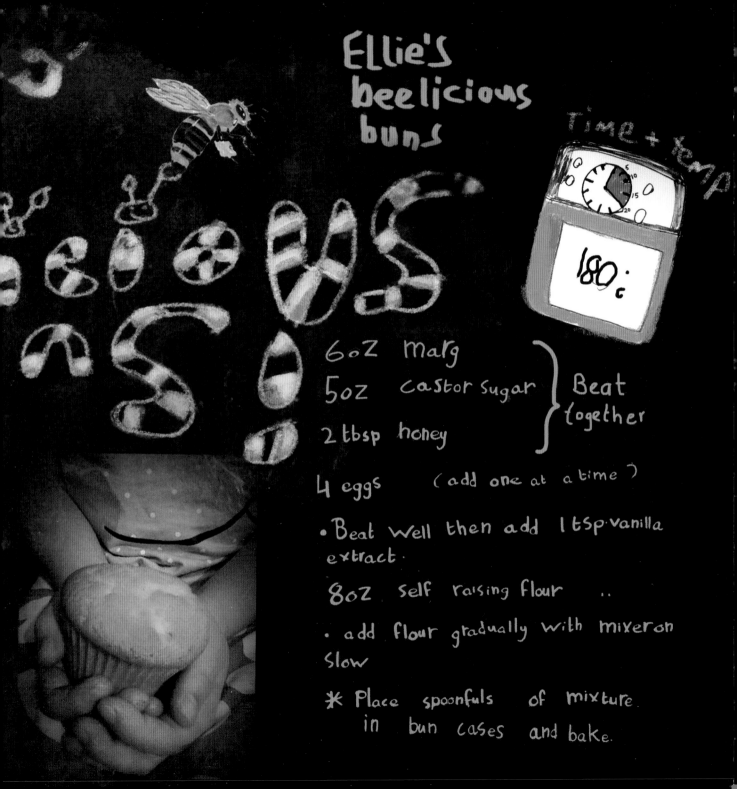

Time + temp

180°c

6oz marg
5oz castor sugar
2 tbsp honey
} Beat together

4 eggs   (add one at a time)

• Beat well then add 1 tsp vanilla extract.

8oz self raising flour   ..

• add flour gradually with mixer on slow

* Place spoonfuls of mixture in bun cases and bake.

Ali's icing for Ellie's beelicious buns

Butter Icing

5 ozs unsalted butter
room temp.
10 ozs icing sugar
(sieved)
1 1/2 tsp of milk

Enough to cover 15 buns

Add all ingredients
together in a mixer and
blend until smooth.
Add colouring paste of
your choice. I prefer
paste to liquid colouring.
Pipe icing onto the top
of buns.

Glace Icing

4 ozs icing sugar (sieved)
2 tbsp water
Enough for 10/12 buns
Place sieved icing sugar in
a bowl. Add water and
colour of your choice and
beat until smooth and
thick enough to cover the
back of a spoon. If too
thick add a very small
amount of water. If too
thin add more sieved icing
sugar. Spread on top of
buns.

Beelicious Smoothie

1 Large pear peeled and chopped
into small pieces
1 peach
1/2 a cup of blueberries
1 cup of natural yoghurt
1 tbsp of local honey

Place all ingredients in a blender and blend
until smooth.
Serves 3 medium glasses.
Beelicious!

Strawberry, Banana & Honey Smoothie

1 banana
1 cup of fresh or frozen
strawberries
1 cup of low fat yoghurt
1 tbsp of local honey

Beelitz it in a blender and enjoy.

Orange, Honey, and Berr[y]
Smoothie.

2 Oranges peeled, pitted an[d]
cut into chunks
1 cup of Blueberries
1 cup of Raspberries
1 tbsp of Honey.
1 cup of yoghurt

Blend together until
smooth and serve.

Serves 3 medium glasse[s]

Yum Yum!

Delicious Fried Bananas in Honey

2 Bananas, halved
2 tbsp of local honey
Knob of butter

Pre heat a frying pan on moderate heat
Roll the bananas in honey until coated
Place butter in pan
Add bananas
Cook until golden brown
Serve with your favourite ice crea

serves 2 people

Yummy Yummy!

A honey bee can fly for up to six miles, and as fast as 15 miles per hour

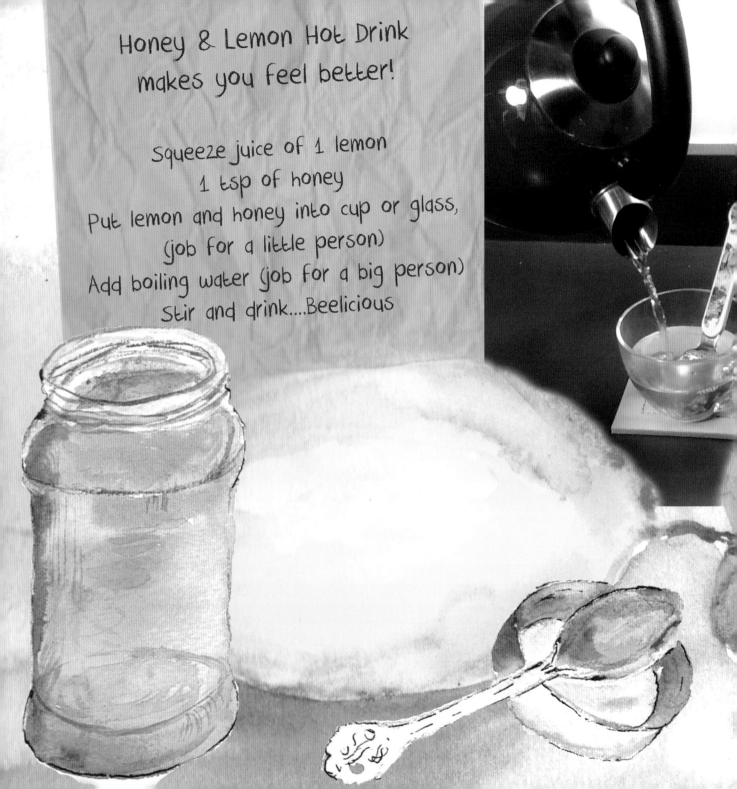

Honey & Lemon Hot Drink
makes you feel better!

Squeeze juice of 1 lemon
1 tsp of honey
Put lemon and honey into cup or glass,
(job for a little person)
Add boiling water (job for a big person)
Stir and drink....Beelicious

The Honey Bee has been
around for
millions of years

cute decoration
for cakes and
cupcakes

you will need →

fondant
icing

dark
chocolate

flak
Alm

Hilary's
Bees

Roll into
Bee shape!

melt choc
add stripes
using stick

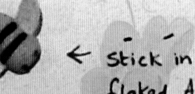

← stick in
flaked Almonds
for the wings .... watch them

don't forget
eyes and smile
:)

cocktail
stick

A honey bee is an AMAZING insect... some more facts.

There are three types of bees in a hive, the queen, the worker and the drone.

It is the colony of bees in the hive who decide on their queen.

The queen rules the colony and as long as she reigns she will be the only bee to lay eggs. The queen bee lives for about 2-3 years

The worker bees are all female. Worker bees do all the work, they clean the hive, feed the queen, collect pollen and nectar. Worker bees convert nectar to honey.

Only worker bees sting, and only if they feel threatened, and they die once they sting.

Worker bees live for 6 to 8 weeks.

The drones are male. They do not work at all, they have no stinger, and their
purpose is to mate with the queen.

A honey bee is the only insect that produces food eaten by man.

Honey bees are vital as pollinators. As bees travel from blossom to blossom in search of nectar, they transfer pollen from plant to plant, thus fertilizing the plants and enabling them to bear fruit.

During winter honey bees feed on the honey they collected during the warmer months. They form a tight cluster in the hive to keep the queen and themselves warm.

Honey bees communicate with each other by dancing. They do a dance which alerts other bees to where nectar and pollen is located - this dance explains direction and distance.

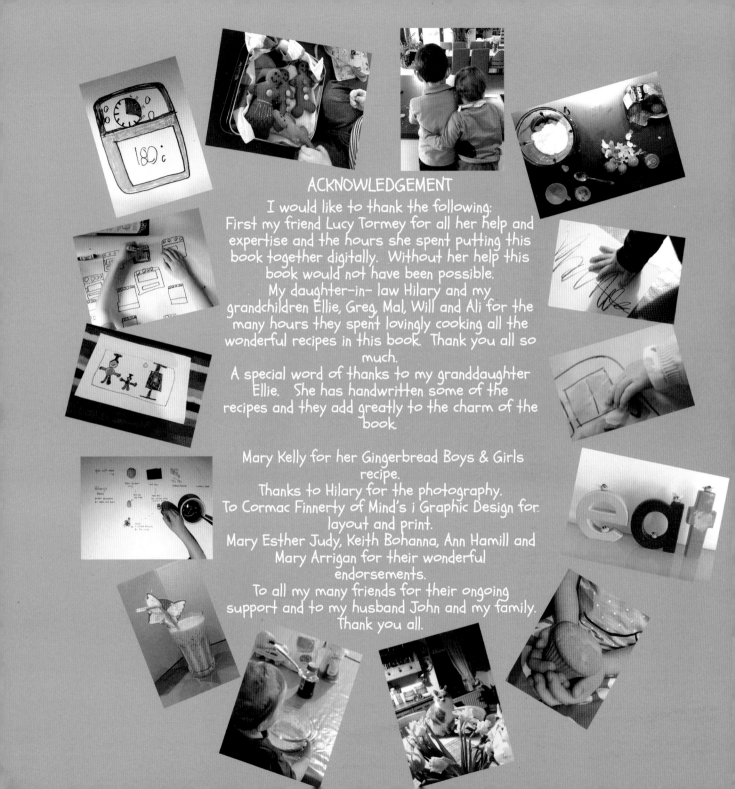

ACKNOWLEDGEMENT

I would like to thank the following:
First my friend Lucy Tormey for all her help and expertise and the hours she spent putting this book together digitally. Without her help this book would not have been possible.

My daughter-in-law Hilary and my grandchildren Ellie, Greg, Mal, Will and Ali for the many hours they spent lovingly cooking all the wonderful recipes in this book. Thank you all so much.

A special word of thanks to my granddaughter Ellie. She has handwritten some of the recipes and they add greatly to the charm of the book

Mary Kelly for her Gingerbread Boys & Girls recipe.
Thanks to Hilary for the photography.
To Cormac Finnerty of Mind's i Graphic Design for layout and print.
Mary Esther Judy, Keith Bohanna, Ann Hamill and Mary Arrigan for their wonderful endorsements.
To all my many friends for their ongoing support and to my husband John and my family. Thank you all.